Field Guide for End Days

poems by

Nishat Ahmed

Finishing Line Press
Georgetown, Kentucky

Field Guide for End Days

*"The only thing I haven't done yet is die
and it's me and my plus one at the afterlife"*

—Fall Out Boy, "Thriller"

Copyright © 2020 by Nishat Ahmed
ISBN 978-1-64662-226-9 First Edition
All rights reserved under International and Pan-American Copyright Conventions. No part of this book may be reproduced in any manner whatsoever without written permission from the publisher, except in the case of brief quotations embodied in critical articles and reviews.

ACKNOWLEDGMENTS

These poems appear nowhere besides this book, and for a long time I was afraid that they would not appear here either. I would first and foremost, like to thank my wonderful professors and mentors at Old Dominion University in no particular order: Luisa A. Igloria, Tim Seibles, and Remica Bingham-Risher. Thank you for looking at these poems in their fresh and young states and for guiding my voice when it felt lost. Thank you for believing in these poems.

Publisher: Leah Maines
Editor: Christen Kincaid
Cover Art: Stephanie Holliger
Author Photo: Camille Gay
Cover Design: Elizabeth Maines McCleavy

Printed in the USA on acid-free paper.
Order online: www.finishinglinepress.com
          also available on amazon.com

                Author inquiries and mail orders:
                       Finishing Line Press
                         P. O. Box 1626
                 Georgetown, Kentucky 40324
                           U. S. A.

Table of Contents

God wanted us in America 1
Field Guide for End Days (Shooter) 2
Sunday Afternoons 3
At a Funeral the Summer I was Eight 4
Last Love Letter to Saturn 5
Transmissions from The Aftersleep No. 1 6
Field Guide for End Days (Places) 7
In Portland, We watch a Man get arrested during Dinner
    at Denny's 8
Field Guide for End Days (Flashlight) 10
Open Letter to Tonya Harding 11
Cardinal as Metaphor for Body Crossing State Lines 12
Field Guide for End Days (Mother) 13
After Abel's Death, the Raven Comes to Me 14
Transmissions from The Aftersleep No. 2 15
Aubade for Lineage Underground/Underwater 16
Field Guide for End Days (Captain) 17
Charon Over the Concrete 18
A Litany that is just Your Name, Repeated 19
Field Guide for End Days (Dear god) 20
[…] 21
It Rained Gold in Virginia 22
And the Kites All Looked like Stingrays in the Sky 23
Field Guide for End Days (Fire) 24
Below Vesuvius 25
Thrush ('thrəsh) 26
Hemayet 27
Field Guide for End Days (Forgotten) 29
my heart is an island that remembers 30
Field Guide for Dreams 31
Destruction Myth 32
Field Guide for End Days (Light) 33

God wanted us in America

my father says at the dinner table,
the fork in his hand clanking
against the ceramic plate.

We stop our eating and listen
to his journey to this country,
mustard oil and *moshla* thick

on our fingers. *The ocean
was below me, I was eighteen
and alone on a plane for the first time.*

*Halfway over the Atlantic, the captain
told us to pray. An engine had blown
and to salvage the flight, they were going*

*to dump the oil. From the window
I watched the dark stream and man,
I started praying for everything.*

*Thanks god, yes, thanks god
he wanted me to make it.
So if anyone tells you*

*you don't belong in America,
you tell them that god himself
brought you here.*

Field Guide for End Days

There is an active shooter
in your vicinity. His name
is America and he is hell bent

on putting a bullet in every
country. What is home but a place
where nothing can find you?

Take shelter. The planes are falling.
Children wish on their flaming streaks—
please, god, don't let the world sink.

Have you heard the news?
We are guilty of all the good
we have never done.

This life is coming for us
like a hammer, like a gavel.
Close your eyes

and imagine you could live
your life over again.
It's too late for that, isn't it?

Sunday Afternoons

Eggplants sizzle
in mustard oil
and cumin seeds.

Our grandmother
wipes sweat
from her brow,

smears it
with paprika
and turmeric

by accident. The hunger
grumbles in our bellies,
the smell igniting

memory on our tongues.
From her head,
we watch a strand

of hair drift
into the pan but
we will eat anyway.

At a Funeral the Summer I was Eight

You told me we bury
bodies like seeds,
that we bloom
into daisies long
after. But what now,

before you're lowered into cold,
dead earth? What happens when you die
in Chicago's winter? Where sparrows and grackles shiver
in silence, and light—shrouded and mangled
in the morning mist—dodges everything
save for the hyacinth and baby's breath on your casket.

The *imam* mutters something in Arabic (probably a prayer)
but I can't understand him or why god needed you
as a flower so soon. The shovels ring
like rusted bells. Everyone's eyes wear crowns of ice.
What could be colder in our bodies
than the grief we can't make space for?

Maybe this is why the dirt won't give way to pocket you.
No space left on this planet for flowers.

Last Love Letter to Saturn

> *On September 15th, 2017, NASA space orbiter and probe, Cassini-Huygens, began the Grand Finale phase of its mission, intentionally plummeting towards and burning up in Saturn's atmosphere in response to exhausted fuel levels.*

I am in your arms. Time may stop
and start, I don't notice.

This is love.
I spent a third of my life

finding you; the rest is history
man will speak of long after

your dazzling charms, your aurin
hair tousled by your gales, have me.

More than a decade I ached for you
to touch me. I welcome the heat,

straddled by you, muscles shimmering,
bones made of comet and crushing.

Maybe our children will rollick
over your moons, glimmer in light

that dressed my skin.
Maybe we can run to Andromeda.

I no longer have to imagine;
I pull from your tongue all possibility.

Here, passing through your glowing rings,
my next mark will be your mouth.

Transmissions from the Aftersleep No. 1

Assalamualaikum. Why have you come?
My grandfather welcomes me
with the traditional greeting.

Waalaikumsalaam I say back.
I'm not exactly sure why.
To learn? I know little, and I'm afraid.

Here, on the other side of dreams
where the dead mill around
my grandfather has been waiting for me.

His beard tessellated with shades
of gray looks the same as
pictures I grew up staring at.

He gestures almost to himself,
a sign allowing questions.
Does it hurt?

*Of course it does. What thing would ever
want to leave the living?*
What happens after?

What are we to do while we are alive?
My grandfather pulls a book off a shelf
I didn't realize was there.

Life is just a catalogue for death.
Should I be scared?
Are you afraid of the next breath you take?

Could that stop you from breathing?
My grandfather opens the book.

Field Guide for End Days

take what made you
put it in a jar—

the mechanical bird
pissing oil into the ocean

the tongue fumbling
over first words

the two freckles
on your right hand

spaced close enough
they might be mistaken

for binary stars—
shut the lid tight

kiss the glass
how cool is it

against your lips?
lock all the doors

crawl under your bed
hold the jar close

& hope   because
there are places where

you can't hide & then
there are places where

god can't touch us

In Portland, We watch a Man get arrested during Dinner at Denny's

and at first we were laughing when he said
I promise I'll pay next week,
then we get a glimpse of his shirt:

a walk raising money for Alzheimer's.
So we get quieter,
maybe he's just forgotten

and I keep forking down my skillet.
Will spins yarns from college but pauses
when we hear the man scream

You bitch! to the manager
who's locked the door and is looking
at the security guard on the phone

with the cops. They send two cars,
three officers, sit the man down.
It's here we ask what he owes,

thinking an easy ten bucks
can keep him from a cell.
But the waitress says

This is the third time he's done this,
so we go back to chattering,
I wolf down what's left of Courtney's pancakes—

mountain of whipped cream and all—
watching as the officers put the man's hands
behind his back. Though he's called

someone a bitch, and though he's skipped
his check three times,
I still consider asking the waitress

if I can curb his debt—
all three hungry checks—because
often, I've scarfed down

a can of chickpeas
called it breakfast,
lunch and dinner.

I've sat at a table
with a plate of food thinking
of how seldom I have a plate of food,

thinking about my empty stomach
and not thinking
of my wallet void of coin.

But my memory of hunger
is not enough to ignite
my engine of courage.

I watch the officers lead the man out
into the maw of a cruiser's backseat.
Butter and cream melt on my tongue.

peace, comfort

Field Guide for End Days

I was afraid of the dark or of dying or both,
so I'd fall asleep holding a flashlight.

In summer I hold my breath when fireflies blink,
I know the dead speak code in flashing lights.

Dear god, if you're listening to me,
flash lightning once.

An observation about death: I once saw a tree and then
saw where it once was. In between, lightning flashed.

I heard the world was ending. I heard something
was coming to swallow the sun. Did you pack your flashlight?

Open Letter to Tonya Harding

Dear Tonya, how did it feel to have your life robbed by men? Do you believe we are made for something? Did you ever touch the ice again after it was taken from you? Tonya, when your blades carve ice, does it feel like you can cut anything? There must be a place where everyone knows their way to a crown. There must be a place where it can be broken. Tonya, tell me of the anger it takes to make a child into a champion. Tell me this hurt is worth it even though you know it isn't. Tell me you prayed between the second and third Axel even though you didn't. Tonya, what earthly means do we give up for a heaven of love? Is there a grace beyond the body on a blade moving through time? What is it like to watch your future fizzle on a tv screen? To know the world is watching it, too? Why do I feel like I need you? *Why? Why? Why?* Tonya, I believe it wasn't you but, Tonya, tell me the truth. If you could break god's kneecaps, would you do it?

brote opponents' kneecaps

Cardinal as Metaphor for Body Crossing State Lines

I remember seeing my first cardinal. It was winter,
the first I had ever spent in my new home. Among
the stark skeletons of the forest preserve, a cardinal flashed
its red, fluttering between snow-crusted branches.
A heartbeat fighting to stay warm.

–

Most cardinals from the midwest are not migratory.
Most mate for life.
The cardinal holds *state bird* for the most states
(Seven of them, to be precise),
all the way from the midwest
to the east coast—Illinois to Virginia.

–

There's a version of this story where
the cardinal stays in Chicago,
and the winter plucks every fruit and every leaf
and every branch off the trees until there is nowhere
to hide from the snow.

–

My first winter in Virginia I did not see a single cardinal.
I think they knew it was going to snow here, too.
I think they knew this was a place where
only silly birds come to die.

–

There's a version of this story where
the bird is both in Chicago and not.
It is March. It is still winter.
I'm going to miss myself
and I won't,
silly bird.

Field Guide for End Days

I. One day your mother
put you down
and never picked you
back up again.

II. One day Heidi
went to sleep
and never woke
up again.

III. Tell me it isn't strange
how we do
so many things
for the last time.

IV. One day my brother
said *yeah, I'll quit smoking,*
and I believe he will
when his lungs give up.

V. One day god said
I'll be right back
and that's the last time
we ever heard from them.

VI. Tell me it's strange
to say *I'll love you
forever* when death
pinches every tongue.

After Abel's Death, the Raven Comes to Me

by the windowsill / that corvus croon echoing again / and again / and again like the old stories said / *thrice the caw opens death's jaw* / so it has come for me / I dream in whatever season I want / the air comes to me / still sinister / some omen in the form of graceless snow / it's only July / I kissed my lover once / I bled strawberry juice / I don't care if it's summer / I wrap myself in cloth / and more cloth and maybe / a little shame and more cloth / can we sweat it out / the large stuff? / the heavy years? / a forewarned solstice / December's come recklessly / I must maim myself / for I have already / maimed the brother / of my blood / oh / what have I done? / oh brother / how I have loved thee / oh brother / tell me how love / makes a monster of us all / may these dark wings / forgive me / may my teeth fall / to the earth like seeds / I want to return the rust / to the stars where particles come from / molt this shell casing my skin / calcium cocoon / I am going to die one day / if I do / don't tell me what happens next / if I don't / go ahead, spoil the ending

Transmissions from the Aftersleep No. 2

The book my grandfather opens is empty.
    He points to a page, also empty, and says
        Read this.   I can't see anything.

Of course you cannot, it is the language of death.
    Closing the book, he returns it
        to the shelf with no other books.

How do I learn to speak it?
    How did you learn to speak our tongue?
        Listening to mom, and dad, and grandma.

So how will you learn this language?
    Listening? Listening to death? How do you do that?
        How? How can you stop? How can you ever stop?

Aubade for Lineage Underground/Underwater

What I know of who I am
is that I do not know much.

Barisal is my parents' home province,
sprawling shorter than a pen cap on the map.

To name my grandparents is to name
every leaf of family history I can touch.

From the earth, the sky above my parents'
village is flooded with stars named after the dead.

From space, the tin roofs huddled by the river
are tombstones guarding the water.

Field Guide for End Days

> *"They say the captain goes down with the ship,*
> *so when the world ends, will god go down with it?"*
> —Fall Out Boy, "What a Catch, Donnie"

this is your captain   speaking
   hello, my name is   god,   my name is
whatever you need it   to be
i am just here   to let you know
   we will be crashing soon
every plane   is falling   from the sky
and we   are the first to land
 there will be no survivors
   that was never the plan
i never promised you   would make it
out of here   alive   i only promised
   a chance   if you have   anything
to say please   say it now
 you all have time   for one phone call
      i used mine to tell you this

Charon over the Concrete

These days the rain
        takes no notice—
drowning some,
        parching others;

my umbrella a taxi
        for moths and other
small beings, my body
        a ferry across the river

that was once a sidewalk,
        flooded with milkweeds
and asters uprooted
        from the eroding soil.

I wiggle my hand
        in the wet fabric
until the cool metal
        of a quarter grazes my thumb,

checking my pockets
        to make sure I have enough
to bring these shells
        to the next life.

A Litany that Is just Your Name, Repeated

   lover   darling   sweetness   Camille
that soundless sound   between wind

and chime   it is just your name
  bee balm   goldenrod garden's

light   look   how the switchgrass
   twitches   at the hand   of the breeze

 knees pocked with summer's dirt
a flower   you weren't named after

  the storm for which you were
your name   a moon in my throat

night   turns to prayer
   dawn   a river of honey

Field Guide for End Days

Dear god, I think you've got the scale wrong, took the wrong people. Is it always warm where you are and is the sun always shining? Do you sit at a table with your buds and kick it lazy and cool? Who's drinking what? Who's shouldering the tab? Is it a cold beer kissed with lime kind of summer night? Have you bet the house on your pocket sevens and the small hope that someone's listening to you? Dear god, do you get too drunk and get careless with who goes and who stays? Dear god, do you even know my name? Or the names of all the things you've created? Dear god, are you out there? Dear god, are you listening? Dear god, why am I so sad? Did you make me this way? Did you make all my friends this way? All my lovers? Why do we lose our minds at night? Why do I want to die? Why can't you save me? Why did my friends want to die? Why didn't you save them? I used to pray and I used to hold your name like the only coin I had, and I held it safe and close in my pocket, my fingers always thumbing the grooves and ridges. Dear god, can I spend you for something better? If you've forgotten my name, am I allowed to forget yours? Dear god, do you ever hurt? And if you do, why? Dear god what's your favorite song? And is it the one you want to die to? Dear god, I know you can hear me talking. Dear god, why don't you ever talk back?

[...]

there are days where
the love feels so great
there is no earth
large enough to hold it

there are pockets
of the heart
still waiting
to be heard

the language we use
shapes the way
love moves
around us

love makes the body
a field that must
be burned
so it can grow again

i have seen heaven
and it looks
like
this

there are nights where
the love feels so small
i mistake salt grains
for stars

there is a hunger
we fear so deeply
we keep it
sleeping

most days
i am afraid
i have misplaced
my tongue

i imagined a future
without you
and it touched my heart
like death

i have seen hell
and it looks
like
this

It Rained Gold in Virginia

A cloud of pollen coating cars, windows, streets;
local apiologists said *the bees will have honey*

for years. An old man died, staring up as it fell, his mouth
agape like a chicken catching rain, tongue now sticky like honey.

I heard his last words were *look at the lord's message,*
garbled by the pollen filling his throat, *cometh the lord's honey.*

For weeks we hid indoors. The bees abandoned their hives,
swarming over every covered surface that might bring them honey.

The sky, once bluer than the waters of our dreams, now shimmering
in the aurum light of a new sun, wears a shawl the color of honey.

Weeks turn to years, the world gummy and glossed in gold film.
We learn how to live off what the bees have given us: honey

in our coffee and cakes, salads dressed in salt, oil, paprika
and that infinite glue, scientists learn to make fuel out of honey.

We build temples for the bees to frolic in. The queens of each colony
enjoy their own little rooms with small thimbles full of honey,

licking the ever-falling pollen from their wings and antennae,
like children do the first time their tongues touch honey.

And the Kites All Looked like Stingrays in the Sky

bobbing above us / on Lake Michigan's shore, / and it was so hot that I forget / where the sky ended, / where the water began. / Behind us Chicago doted noisily, / the rumbling tracks and chorus of horns, / if you put an ear to the sand you could hear the earth / tremble beneath thousands of feet. And that night / my friends and I slid through the grid / until we found a dive bar with a live band / playing cheap covers of radio hits. / Maybe it was Alex, / or maybe it was Logan, / bought the rounds of margaritas for the fires / sitting in our throats, / and we sipped down a panacea for the summer / where it seemed like we were always thirsty, / and another round for the summer / where the group lost a mother / or an old high school friend. / And when the band ended the night / with an off-key rendition of an Ed Sheeran hit, / we spilled out the bar the way the coins do / from fraying pockets. And there, / under the yellow smog / of the city lights, maybe it was Alex, / maybe it was Logan, / looked up and said / *my god, / I can see all the stars.*

Field Guide for End Days

> *In the sixth month / of a disastrous reign in the house of money // in the street of money in the city of money in the country of money, / our great country of money, we (forgive us) // lived happily during the war.*
> —Ilya Kaminsky

the bombs are falling and the walls of money are caving in but we built our houses out of paper and our people out of paper and we cut down entire countries of trees just to make empires out of paper and its so ironic now that the world is on fire everything is on fire the bombs are on fire and the fire on the bombs are on fire and the fire of the bombs that are on fire are also on fire and the paper people in their paper castles are also on fire i shake your hand *hi hello how are you burning today* and you grin back and shake my hand and say *oh fine burning just fine* and where our palms touch there is for a moment a pause and some smoke but then of course there is fire again and who is dropping the bombs and why isnt there a place to take shelter why arent the leaders of our countries doing anything about the fire oh its because they are on fire too and they are made of paper too and they want more walls of money which are if you would believe it made of paper and that paper is on fire too and honestly its hard to remember anything when our brains are on fire but i think they told us in school once that paper is a very flammable substance and when we played rock paper scissors none of us believed paper could actually beat rock and honestly i think rock would have been able to keep us from the fire and no please dont interrupt me to ask me if this is hell thats a stupid question of course this isnt hell this is hell and then some anyways it seems like we were taught at a pretty young age that paper is pretty weak and we were taught the dangers of fire too so i guess we should have known this would happen and if we knew this would happen and did it anyway i guess its safe to say that we deserved all of this

Below Vesuvius

The bones of Pompeii
        hide near the flesh of Naples,
    even in death somehow rendered living
by the blood of people cycling in and out
    of ruin—buildings and bodies

embalmed by the black dust.
    The shells of life so out of place
in the thriving metropolis wedged
        against thickets of fig trees and pine.
  The caldera's cracked maw

  yawns, smoke and magma curdle
in its throat. Near the drop of the rocky lip, a man below,
      his feet balanced between earth
and death—one little breath
    of air is all it would take to send him—

It's only the two of us. I can't help
    but think how easy it'd be to slink over, nudge him
into emptiness. No one else knowing
    except me. This man alive only
like a city preserved in the ash of my memory.

Thrush ('thrəsh)

       I.
n., in the eastern
half of the states, browned
feathers, throat like a flute—
ee-oh-lay flutters the song
through the bramble sailing
off every cinnamon leaf.
On the forest floor, thrush
foraging for invertebrate prey,
occasionally peering up,
scanning the sky, wings
splayed out like a crown, letting
the puff of white on its chest
gleam like a beacon.

      II.
n., in the eastern
half of the mouth, too much
beer and wine on weekends,
too much trying to wash out
loneliness settling
like sores on the tongue.
Prodded by the teeth
like a sharp crown,
tongue begging for mercy,
teeth begging for the tongue
to speak, rather than drink,
yellowed, and rotting and angry,
thinking about when
they gleamed new and naked
like the first beams of light.

Hemayet

A wreath of geese crown the thumbprint of the sun.
The light seems sharper and dimmer against the canvas of snowfall.
I want to know you so I pack a fistful into my beard,
trying to paint my black hair white and gray. For a moment it feels like
    remembering,
the cold shocking the skin underneath. What little I have of you is this:

Your name, *Hemayet*, which I know as my brother's name before yours.
And even then I wonder if that really is yours, as your father died
    before you were two,
your mother by the time you were six. Was it granted to you by your
    parents?
Or your school teacher whose son you tutored in exchange for food
    and home?
Or your spiritual teacher who, for nine years, versed you in the ways
    of Allah?
Even in death, do you sometimes have trouble remembering?

Your face, whose stern, tender eyes kept vigil
in my *chachu's* Chicago apartment, that face I see in my all dreams,
your figure draped in white cloth. Some nights in the mirror,
I see the ghost of you in myself and I reach for my cheek.

Your voice, which if I ever could hear you speak,
I would imagine sounded like that of the cab driver
who, too, was from Bangladesh and, upon hearing I was a poet,
began to sing to me Tagore's poems in our mother tongue.

And I wonder how often you sang those poems too,
or if you sang them at all, or if your tongue spent more time
singing *surrahs* than songs, and I wonder if you'd agree with me
when I say poems are prayers and when I touch the page
I am trying to plead with god, and most of all I wonder if you'd be
    proud of me

for making it this far, or if because I am no longer a servant of Allah,
I serve no purpose to you. But that must be my own insecurity
muddling the truth because on the phone when I ask my father
to tell me your story he says *all he ever did was preach tolerance and
    love,*

and when I tell him I've been seeing you in my dreams and in cab
    drivers
he starts crying but moves away from the speaker hoping I can't hear.
Between breaths my father says this is normal, that you have so much
    power
you are a man who is mortal and is not. And we both sit with this, the
    static
buzzing in our ears before he says *you have his blood.*

Field Guide for End Days

Trace the bodies of the loves
you have forgotten.

There can be no forgiveness
for that which we've forgotten.

My mother had a name before she gave me one,
one that I have forgotten.

The living become dead while living
if they are forgotten.

I'm supposed to tell you something about how to survive
the end of the world, but I've forgotten.

How important can anything be
if it's forgotten?

my heart is an island that remembers

when it was a continent
when the borders were made
by oceans not by bullets
or bombs my heart is both
a wreck and wreckage
eventually everything
will be swallowed
by the sea
what i mean to say is
the heart is both the wave
the shore
water and salt
what i mean to say is
the country whose
language first rested
on my tongue
is slowly dissolving
in the mouth of the sea
being bit away by the teeth
of the mountains
when i tell my children of home
they will not know
what to imagine
the heat of the jungle
the reprieve of the river
as foreign to them
as the words i speak
in the maps of the future
there will be a hole the size of a country
and everywhere the water
everywhere the water

Field Guide for Dreams

my paternal grandfather died shortly after i met him   i was a year old
his pillowy gray beard   all i remember   every person seen in a dream
living or dead   is dead   the first time i heard my grandfather's
voice was at seven on a cassette tape of him praying   my father
played it on the anniversary of his death   it was the only day
of the year i saw him cry   clocks do not work   in dreams
books cannot be read   because of this   the dead can touch us
the bangla i speak and the bangla my grandfather speaks are two
different tongues   i dreamt in black and white until i was nine
my grandfather's name is Hemayet   no recollection of origin
no last name   he built our village with his bare hands
in the last sleep   i see him in   i ask him   what is it like to die?
and he says   it is kind of like dreaming

Destruction Myth

I fear my most tender days were behind me
long before I met you. But here I am,
dripping honey into my coffee,
for you make the most bitter fruit, sweet.
And it is no mistake I put honey here,
for honey alone could sustain a body
starved of everything else.
And I know during the end days
when the rice paddies of Bangladesh
to the fields of soybeans and corn in Illinois
have all been razed by locusts or flames,
we will climb every tree to find what little is left
to live on. From the homes of bees
we will shake everything into our throats;
wings, stingers, honey and all and with our swollen tongues
we will recite the words *waaax* and *hiiive* and *cooomb*
elongated and bloated as if it were the first time
we had found a language for our hurt and desire.
And finally, after all the world is ash and our sky
is no longer sullied by man's polluted light, every star
there ever was shall burn above us, hungry and gold.
And under the shimmering cosmic pollen
of forever's first spring, you will ask *will you have me?*
and I will say yes, and yes again,
until god's fingers snuff every mote of light.

Field Guide for End Days

this poem has already been written   and still i must   recite it again
    every act of naming is   an act of god   every act of loving
is an act   of god   we have been so wrong   this is heaven
and we have been wasting   our time bickering   over things like
    gold and silver   honey and meat   we have been   so wrong
this   is hell   and i have been   burning   just to tell you this
   if you can remember   all the names   of the people you have
    ever loved   even when the light   has swallowed us
          then maybe   it was worth the living

Additional Acknowledgements

To the many living writers of color I have looked up to in working on and through poems; Kaveh Akbar, Ocean Vuong, Hanif Abdurraqib, Amanda Galvan Huynh (hi mom), Nicole Sealey, Tracy K. Smith, Ross Gay, Tarfia Faizullah, Claudia Rankine, Donika Kelly, Chris Santiago, Mai Der Vang, Angel Nafis, Safia Elhillo, Danez Smith, Jericho Brown, Chen Chen, Fatimah Asghar, José Olivarez, Franny Choi, Sarah Kay, and John Murillo, your work has been a beacon. I know there are more names I have not read yet to add to this list. For that abundance, I am grateful.

Unending gratitude for my family, for the work they have put in, for what they have given up so I could have. These poems are my way of saying *I love you* and also my way of saying *thank you*. I know it is not easy to raise a writer. Thank you for doing it anyway.

Julie Price, bless you for telling a confused and scared twenty-year-old *if you do anything else but writing with your life, you're making a mistake.*

Fall Out Boy forever.

A deep thank you to my friends, both the ones that have made it this far and the ones that have not. You all remind me what it means to be human, especially the squad. You know who you are. To small ships and big ships.

I would also like to thank my best friend, Kelsey Wort, for her unwavering belief in my writing and my humanity. Thank you for erasing my second guesses and for your infinite well of wisdom. Without you, I would not be here.

And of course, of course, thank you to my love, Camille. If there is a point to all of this, it is you. When the end days come, I hope I still have the honor of being by your side. All that I am has been practice in being yours. Thank you for loving me.

Nishat Ahmed is a Bangladeshi-American residing in the Midwest. He is an Illinois native with a deep love for Fall Out Boy, *The Notebook* and Chipotle. He received his MFA in poetry from Old Dominion University. His work blends the power of the lyric with the urgency of punk confessionalism. He wants you to know that if there is something worth writing about, worth living for, it is love.

His work has been published by *Sobotka, Words Dance, The Mochila Review, Blue Agave, The Academy of American Poets, The Tampa Review*, and has been performed at TEDxUIUC and AWP. His second chapbook, *Brown Boy*, is forthcoming from Porkbelly Press.